400/
mcp

WORKING STEAM
Rebuilt Royal Scots

Ian Allan
60th ANNIVERSARY

THE THAMES-CLYDE EXPRESS

46162

Gavin Morrison

Introduction

I am delighted to have this opportunity to present this photographic tribute to the rebuilt 'Royal Scots'. Officially they were known as 'converted Royal Scots', but as the only original parts left from the parallel-boilered locomotives were the cab, wheels, frames and tenders, I think 'rebuilt' is a more accurate description.

I have always had a particular interest in these locomotives, especially the first rebuilds to be allocated to Leeds Holbeck shed, as I still clearly remember walking to the end of the platform at Leeds City station in 1943, armed with my Ian Allan *ABC of LMS Locomotives* (which I still have), to see which locomotive was going to haul my father and me to Glasgow St Enoch on the 10.35am working. I was extremely surprised to see No 6103 *Royal Scots Fusilier* at the head of the train, looking like nothing I could find in my 'ABC', but all was revealed in due course.

The first of the class to be rebuilt was indeed No 6103 *Royal Scots Fusilier*, in June 1943, after authorisation had been given for an initial batch of 20 to be done. In 1942 two 'Jubilees' had been rebuilt and were almost identical to the rebuilt 'Royal Scots'; in fact, at one time it was thought that all the 'Jubilees', 'Patriots' and 'Scots' should be rebuilt. As it turned out only two 'Jubilees' were done, 18 'Patriots' and all the 'Royal Scots'. The programme for the 'Scots' took 13 years to complete, No 46137 *The Prince of Wales' Volunteers (South Lancashire)* finally emerging from Crewe Works in March 1955. The unrebuilt engines had, of course, been given general repairs during this period, and the order in which they were done apparently depended on the state of the locomotives; the unrebuilt locomotives had been giving a considerable amount of trouble and proving expensive to maintain. (The mass rebuilding of 'Jubilees' and 'Patriots' did not proceed because, it is believed, of the introduction of the BR Standards and because only 99 Type 2A boilers were constructed at Crewe.)

Two of the rebuilt 'Scots' — Nos 46162 *Queen's Westminster Rifleman* and 46154 *The Hussar* — took part in the 1948 Locomotive Exchanges, and the late Cecil J. Allen, widely acknowledged as one of the greatest experts at assessing locomotive performance, is quoted as saying: 'Relative to the moderate dimensions and weight, and the simplicity of the design of those 4-6-0s… I should be inclined to rate their best performance above everything else witnessed during the test weeks' — praise indeed from an ex-LNER man.

The rebuilt 'Scots' represented surely one of the most successful rebuilds of any class in Britain, and there were few other designs of comparable size and weight (about 83 tons) that could compete in terms of hauling capabilities. In the late 1940s and 1950s, particularly during the summer months, trains on the West Coast main line regularly loaded to 16 or 17 coaches, which seemed to present little problem to a good engine south of Crewe; 'Scots' are recorded as taking trains of 16 coaches (totalling 530 tons gross) up the bank out of Crewe to Madeley Summit and passing it at 50mph. In the author's opinion they were also extremely handsome locomotives, particularly before the fitting of the smoke-deflectors and when painted in the LMS's 1946 style of gloss black with maroon and straw lining, and also in the British Railways lined-black livery.

Almost all locomotive designs had a weakness — some more than others — and the rebuilt 'Scots' were no exception. They tended to be rather rough riders — in fact very rough when due for overhaul. From my own very limited experience of footplate rides on the class, not only were they rough but they also seemed also to roll, giving me (at least) the impression of being rather top-heavy, but their ability to pull heavy trains economically was never in doubt.

In rebuilt form the 'Scots' were allocated to all the main sheds from Polmadie to Camden and performed virtually any express-passenger duty that existed on the London Midland's Western Division. Holyhead had its own small allocation for working the Irish Mail trains, while the Leeds Holbeck engines seldom wandered from their duties between Leeds and Glasgow via the Settle & Carlisle and Glasgow & South Western lines. This situation continued until the very late 1950s and early 1960s, when the English Electric Type 4 diesels appeared on the West Coast route, which saw the class moving to new areas. Many had a short spell on the expresses on the Midland

First published 2002

ISBN 0 7110 2883 4

Published by Ian Allan Publishing

an imprint of Ian Allan Publishing Ltd, Hersham, Surrey KT12 4RG.
Printed by Ian Allan Printing Ltd, Hersham, Surrey KT12 4RG.

Code: 0208/B2

line, until again replaced by diesels (this time of the BR/Sulzer Type 4 'Peak' variety). They were almost but not quite totally replaced on the Settle & Carlisle Scottish expresses by Gresley 'A3s', and indeed they shared this work with three 'Britannias' allocated to Holbeck for a few years.

Unfortunately the mileage records are not complete for all 'Royal Scots', particularly for those that finished up on the North Eastern Region. Generally, records are complete to December 1960. It appears that most members of the class achieved just over 2,000,000 miles, except for the Polmadie-allocated locomotives, which probably accumulated the lowest mileages (although their records are complete only to December 1957). The highest *recorded* mileage achieved by an individual locomotive was 2,548,329, reached by No 46133 three months before its withdrawal. Generally the highest annual mileages appear to have been achieved by the locomotives in unrebuilt form in the years just before World War 2, prior to the introduction of the 'Coronation' Pacifics.

December 1962 provided the first major blow to the class, with no fewer than 23 being withdrawn in that month alone. Thereafter the survivors were allocated all over the London Midland Region, mainly for secondary duties, including freight work, along with the rebuilt 'Patriots' and 'Jubilees'. Some even finished up allocated to Annesley shed on the ex-Great Central line for working semi-fasts between Nottingham and Marylebone. Others were put in and out of store and all were generally in a run-down condition, with such unlikely places as Mirfield and Low Moor having an allocation. For such a

famous and fine class there were only a few farewell railtours, and the end finally came in January 1966 when No 46115 *Scots Guardsman* was withdrawn from Carlisle Kingmoor.

What of the future? Two members of the class have been preserved. No 46100 *Royal Scot* is now at Bressingham Museum, where it has been for many years. No 46115 *Scots Guardsman* did make it back onto the main line for two specials in 1978, when based at the Dinting Railway Museum. After Dinting closed the locomotive finished up at Tyseley, and has now moved to The Railway Age, Crewe. I (and, doubtless, many other steam enthusiasts) would be thrilled to see it working again, especially over the Settle–Carlisle line.

Finally, my thanks to the photographers who have made this album possible — good colour slides of rebuilt 'Scots' do not come in their hundreds!

Gavin Morrison
July 2002

Bibliography
Locomotives Illustrated No 1 and No 68, Ian Allan
Power of the Royal Scots by David Jenkinson, Oxford Publishing Co, 1982
Royal Scots of the LMS edited by Douglas Doherty, Ian Allan, 1970
The Book of the Royal Scots, Irwell Press, 1999

Title page: No 46162 *Queen's Westminster Rifleman* has plenty of coal in the tender after being prepared at Holbeck shed Leeds to work the up 'Thames–Clyde Express' on 23 September 1960. It had been transferred away from the West Coast main line to Kentish Town on 7 November 1959 (on loan), having been ousted from its duties by English Electric Type 4 (later Class 40) diesels. Its stay on the Midland main line was brief, the 'Peak' (Class 45) diesels soon replacing steam, so it ended its days at Carlisle Kingmoor shed, being withdrawn in May 1964. Earlier in its career, following rebuilding in January 1948,

this locomotive (together with No 46154 *The Hussar*) was selected for that year's famous locomotive exchanges, achieving some of the finest performances in the trials. *Gavin Morrison*

Below: An official photograph of No 6103 *Royal Scots Fusilier* in plain LMS black livery as it emerged from Crewe Works in 1943 after extensive rebuilding with new taper boiler, double blastpipe and chimney and with redesigned cylinders and valves. *Ian Allan Library*

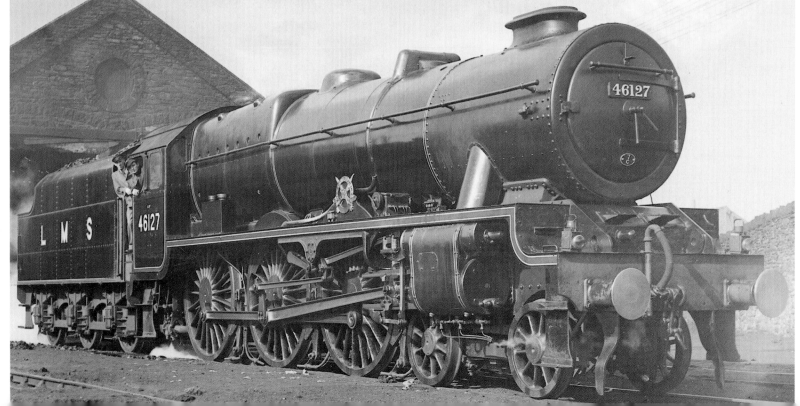

Left: One of the members of the class to receive the 'M' prefix after nationalisation was No M6169 (albeit shown here as 6169M) *The Boy Scout*, seen in plain black livery. *Ian Allan Library*

Below left: An extremely fine study of No 46127 *Old Contemptibles* at its home shed of Holyhead, where it spent several years after rebuilding, working the Irish Mail trains to Euston. Notice its unique nameplate. It is in LMS postwar lined black livery with British Railways number. *Eric Treacy*

Right: An unusual view of No 46101 *Royal Scots Grey* taken inside Camden shed on 9 June 1962. Back in the early 1950s, Camden was its home shed, but by this date it had been transferred to Llandudno Junction (note the 6G shedplate). It was finally moved to Annesley shed on 5 January 1963 for working semi-fasts on the old Great Central Railway. Rebuilt in November 1945, it was withdrawn in August 1963. *G. Rixon*

A fine picture of the first rebuilt 'Royal Scot', No 46103 *Royal Scots Fusilier*, at the buffer-stops of Euston's No 2 arrival platform after working the up 'Lakes Express'. The driver is taking a break whilst waiting for the stock to be removed, after which he will take the locomotive to Camden shed for servicing. At the time of this picture — 14 July 1962 — No 46103 was allocated to Carlisle Upperby. After 15 years at Leeds Holbeck, working the expresses over the Settle &

Carlisle, it had been transferred to Kentish Town on 11 October 1958 and one month later to Trafford Park, Manchester, spending about three years working expresses on the Midland main line; a year was then spent at Saltley before transfer to Carlisle Upperby (its final allocation) on 30 June 1962. It was the first to be rebuilt, in June 1943, and would be withdrawn in December 1962. *G. Rixon*

An interesting picture taken inside Euston shows a rather dirty English Electric Type 4 (later Class 40) on Platform 2 having worked an up express, whilst on Platform 1 rebuilt 'Royal Scot' No 46155 *The Lancer*, in rather cleaner condition, waits to return to Camden or Willesden shed; Camden closed to steam on 9 September 1962 — the year the picture was taken. No 46155 had been rebuilt in August 1950 and would be withdrawn on 12 December 1964 from Holyhead shed. *J. Edgington*

Above: No 46148 *The Manchester Regiment* receives attention on the ash-pits at Camden shed on 22 August 1955. Note the old lion-and-wheel emblem on the tender. It had been one of the last of the class to be rebuilt in July 1954 and would eventually be withdrawn on 14 November 1964 from Holyhead shed. Camden became a diesel depot following closure to steam in 1962. *R. C. Riley*

Right: With smoke, steam and sunlight, No 46125 *3rd Carabinier* makes a fine atmospheric picture on the turntable inside Willesden shed on 6 April 1963. At the beginning of the year it was allocated to Holyhead, and had possibly worked up to London on an Irish Mail relief. It had been an early rebuild — in August 1943 — and lasted until October 1964. *G. Rixon*

For a short period c1963 Newton Heath shed (26A) at Manchester received a small allocation of rebuilt 'Scots', probably for working trains to Blackpool and North Wales, as the London Midland Region's Western Division had plenty of diesels. On 25 May 1963 No 46140 *The King's Royal Rifle Corps* was back on its old stamping-ground, heading an up special (1T81) through Tring Cutting. It had been rebuilt in May 1952 and would be withdrawn in October 1965 from Longsight shed. *T. B. Owen*

Above: The 1.30pm Euston–Blackpool approaches Willesden, having just left Kensal Green Tunnel, headed by No 46167 *The Hertfordshire Regiment* on 10 September 1960, at which time the locomotive was allocated (along with six other members of the class) to Preston. It had been rebuilt in December 1948 and would be withdrawn in April 1964 from Annesley shed. *K. L. Cook*

Right: In plain LMS black livery, No 6169 *The Boy Scout* heads a Euston–Manchester express near Northchurch on 17 June 1947. The locomotive had been rebuilt just over two years earlier and would enjoy another 16 years' service before withdrawal in May 1963; its 9A shedplate denotes allocation to Longsight shed in Manchester. *E. R. Wethersett*

Above: The 12.10pm Manchester London Road (now named Piccadilly)–Euston passes through Tring station on the up fast line on 18 July 1959. The train is hauled by No 46100 *Royal Scot*, which, following its June 1950 rebuild, spent nine years allocated to Camden shed. It was one of the first of the class to be withdrawn, in October 1962, at which time it was allocated to Nottingham (16A) shed. This locomotive is currently preserved at Bressingham. *K. L. Cook / Rail Archive Stephenson*

Right: A dramatic picture of an up express as No 46106 *Gordon Highlander* overflows its tender on Castlethorpe troughs on 30 August 1958. This locomotive was unique amongst the rebuilt 'Scots' in being fitted with British Railways-type smoke-deflectors; it is said these were slightly more efficient than the standard type, which were originally fitted to No 6115 *Scots Guardsman*. No 46106 had been rebuilt in September 1949 and would be withdrawn on 8 December 1962 from Upperby shed. *T. B. Owen*

Left: No 46135 *The East Lancashire Regiment* heads the up 'Emerald Isle Express' over Castlethorpe water-troughs on 30 August 1958. *T. B. Owen*

Above: The wires have not yet been attached to the catenary at Ashton, which is about one mile south of Roade, as No 46142

The York & Lancaster Regiment passes at the head of the up 'Lakes Express' on 1 August 1963. This was an unusual working for a Newton Heath locomotive; possibly it had been diagrammed due to the failure of an English Electric Type 4 diesel. It would be withdrawn in January 1964 and sent to Crewe Works for scrapping the same month. *K. Fairey*

The 9.05am Llandudno–Euston approaches Rugby at 1.34pm on 1 June 1962. This was during the electrification work on the line, when many of the Birmingham services were diverted onto the Great Western route to Paddington. The locomotive is No 46159 *The Royal* *Air Force*, which had been rebuilt in October 1945 and would be withdrawn in December 1962 from Willesden shed. The tender never received the new lion-and-wheel emblem. *P. J. Fitton*

No 46160 *Queen Victoria's Rifleman* passes Lichfield with a down express on 26 June 1959. Three months later, after a 12-year stay at Longsight, this locomotive would be transferred away to Kentish Town. It was withdrawn from Carlisle Kingmoor in May 1965 and scrapped at Motherwell Machinery & Scrap Co Ltd in July 1965. *D. Marriott*

Left: A great picture of No 46120 *Royal Inniskilling Fusilier* on what is believed to be the 9.40am Wolverhampton–Euston, approaching Beechwood Tunnel on the Birmingham–Coventry line. The photograph was taken on 16 April 1961, when the locomotive was allocated to Willesden shed. Rebuilt in November 1944, No 46120 would be withdrawn in July 1963 from Crewe North. *M. Mensing*

Above: Birmingham New Street is the setting for this picture of No 46149 *The Middlesex Regiment*, which had just arrived at Platform 3 with the 10.15am from Liverpool Lime Street and 10.30am Manchester London Road (combined probably at Crewe) on 17 March 1962. The locomotive had been rebuilt in April 1945 and would be withdrawn in August 1963 from Longsight shed. *M. Mensing*

Left: On Sunday 14 September 1958 the 12.10pm Blackpool North–Euston passes near the canal at Milford, southeast of Stafford, headed by No 46157 *The Royal Artilleryman.* This locomotive had been rebuilt in January 1946 and would be withdrawn in January 1964 from Annesley shed. *M. Mensing*

Above: As already mentioned in the Introduction, No 46154 *The Hussar* was one of the two rebuilt 'Scots' to be used in the 1948 locomotive exchanges. It was then tested on the Southern Region and attached to an eight-wheel 'WD' tender to give sufficient water capacity, as the Region did not have water-troughs. On 4 March 1961 it is seen heading the 2pm Liverpool Lime Street–Euston express past Stafford, where the station buildings have been largely demolished due to impending electrification. Rebuilt in March 1948, the locomotive was withdrawn, along with 22 other members of the class, in December 1962, its final allocation being Willesden. *M. Mensing*

Left: The rebuilt 'Scots' were no strangers to the North/West main line — especially the Longsight and Crewe locomotives, which would normally work as far as Pontypool Road, as demonstrated by No 46124 *London Scottish* near Stokesay on 19 August 1961. The locomotive spent 15 of its rebuilt years allocated to Edge Hill, and was frequently seen on trans-Pennine expresses. Rebuilt in December 1943, it would be withdrawn in December 1962 from Carlisle Kingmoor. *D. Penney*

Above: No 46115 *Scots Guardsman* spent 11 of its rebuilt years allocated to Longsight shed in Manchester. It was sent to Carlisle Kingmoor to finish its working days, and was the last to be withdrawn, in January 1966. This picture shows it entering Whitchurch heading for Crewe in 1963. This locomotive had been the first of the rebuilt 'Scots' to be fitted with smoke-deflectors, in late 1947. *D. Penney*

Left: Another photograph of No 46115 *Scots Guardsman*, taken in superb lighting conditions at Crewe North shed on 13 February 1965. *H. Ballantyne*

Below: No 46144 *Honourable Artillery Company* makes a fine sight in the sunshine after its last heavy general repair at Crewe Works on 12 August 1960, when it was allocated to Camden shed (1B). It had been rebuilt in June 1945 and would be withdrawn in January 1964 from Llandudno Junction. *M. Welch*

Below: No 46120 *Royal Inniskilling Fusilier*, still with the old lion-and-wheel emblem on the tender and in fine external condition, waits at the south end of Crewe station to take over an up express in May 1959. It had been rebuilt in November 1944 and was withdrawn in July 1963. *M. Welch*

Right: The rebuilt 'Royal Scots' were regular performers through Chester and were to be seen on the Irish Mail services for around 10 years, until replaced by 'Britannias' in 1954. From then on they appeared on other passenger workings, some eventually being withdrawn from Holyhead and Llandudno Junction sheds. No 46150 *The Life Guardsman* is seen a few miles west of Chester on an up express, probably in the late 1950s. It had been rebuilt in December 1945 and would be withdrawn from Willesden in November 1963 following reallocation there on 22 June that year. *K. Field / Rail Archive Stephenson*

Left: No 46165 *The Ranger (12th London Regt.)* has a 'NOT TO BE MOVED' sign attached to it inside Llandudno Junction shed on 22 June 1963, the day it is recorded as being transferred to Crewe North, after nine months at 6G. Rebuilt in June 1952, it would finally be withdrawn in November 1964 from Annesley shed, having worked services on the ex-Great Central line for nine months. *Gavin Morrison*

Above: Recorded heading north at Madeley Bank, Crewe, in September 1960 at the head of a London–Manchester train, No 46167 *The Hertfordshire Regiment* was originally built in October 1930 and rebuilt in December 1948. The locomotive would be withdrawn in April 1964 and scrapped at Crewe Works the following month. *Derek Cross*

Left: No 46160 *Queen Victoria's Rifleman*, still with nameplate but possibly not the original, shimmers in the sunshine outside Blackpool Central shed on 28 September 1964. It was booked to work a 3pm television train to Glasgow, and returned with a weekend illuminations special. The locomotive had been cleaned by local enthusiasts (one of whom was the photographer), but only the front end and one side received attention. Rebuilt in February 1945, it was the last rebuilt 'Scot' to visit Blackpool Central and would be one of the last to be withdrawn, on 1 May 1965 from Carlisle Kingmoor. Note the diagonal yellow stripe on the cabside, indicating the locomotive was banned from working under the wires south of Crewe. *P. J. Fitton*

Above: Willesden-allocated No 46146 *The Rifle Brigade* has been well cleaned to work Grand National special 1Z64 from Euston to Sefton Arms station via the Bootle Junction line. It is shown on 31 March 1962 on the turntable at Aintree shed, where it was serviced before the return working at 6.10pm, piloted by Stanier Class 5 No 45390 of Edge Hill. An early rebuild, in October 1943, No 46146 would survive at Willesden until December 1962. *P. J. Fitton*

No 46126 *Royal Army Service Corps* heads along the down fast line at Treales, near Kirkham, with a Euston–Blackpool illuminations relief on 30 September 1961. This was the day that Gresley 'A4' No 60022 *Mallard* visited Blackpool with an illuminations special — the real reason for the photographer's presence at the trackside. No 46126 had been rebuilt in June 1945 and would be withdrawn from Annesley shed in October 1963 after working trains on the Great Central. *P. J. Fitton*

Above: The unique rebuild No 46170 *British Legion* heading a Glasgow–Manchester express (1M32) past Skewe Bridge, just south of Preston on 25 August 1962 at 4.43pm. The locomotive looks in reasonable external condition, having had a general repair in September 1961, but it would withdrawn just four months later. The special nameplate stands out well. The locomotive was rebuilt in 1935 (with single chimney) using the frames of the ill-fated experimental *Fury*, its double chimney being fitted around 1948, followed later by the smoke-deflectors. Its final allocation would be to Llandudno Junction shed. *P. J. Fitton*

Left:
The distinctive *British Legion* nameplate attached to No 46170. *G. Rixon*

Above: No 46162 *Queen's Westminster Rifleman* heads an up parcels train past Morecambe South Junction on 13 July 1961, when allocated to Holyhead. Earlier in its career this was one of the two rebuilt 'Scots' which took part in the 1948 Locomotive Exchanges. Its last major repair was in October 1959, and during 1960 it was reallocated five times. Withdrawal would come in May 1964, the locomotive being scrapped by J. N. Connell at Coatbridge that September. *D. Marriott*

Right: Another fine picture at Morecambe South Junction, this time of No 46165 *The Ranger (12th London Regt.)* heading an up express on 13 July 1961. In September 1961 it was transferred to Heaton Mersey, where it stayed for 10 months. Like many others, it finished its days at Annesley shed, working Great Central trains. The end came on 21 November 1964, and it passed to T. W. Ward, Beighton, for scrapping in March 1965. *D. Marriott*

Left: No 46106 *Gordon Highlander*, the only member of the class to be fitted with British Railways' standard smoke-deflectors, approaches Low Gill on a down working on 18 August 1962; the 1-in-75 climb up Shap will present no difficulty to the locomotive with this short (six-coach) train. Rebuilt in September 1949, it would be withdrawn, along with many others, in December 1962, its final allocation being to Carlisle Upperby. *Gavin Morrison*

Above: During the 17 months it was allocated to Newton Heath, Manchester, No 46133 *The Green Howards* passes through the fine scenery of the Lune Gorge at the head of a Manchester–Glasgow express on 18 August 1962. This locomotive had been one of the earlier rebuilds, in July 1944, and spent around 11 years allocated to Leeds Holbeck shed for working the Scottish expresses over the Settle–Carlisle line. It was eventually withdrawn in February 1963 from Newton Heath shed. *Gavin Morrison*

No 46159 *The Royal Air Force* climbs the last mile to Shap Summit
without a trace of exhaust on a very hot 6 August 1960, when it was
allocated to Crewe North shed. *Gavin Morrison*

No 46132 *The King's Regiment, Liverpool* puts up a fine exhaust as it accelerates away from Penrith on the fast downhill section of line to Carlisle. The picture was taken from the B5305 roadbridge just north of the town on 31 May 1963. By this date the locomotive was allocated to Carlisle Upperby, although after the arrival of the English Electric Type 4 diesels it spent two years (November 1959 to October 1961) allocated to Kentish Town for duties on the Midland main line. *Gavin Morrison*

Above: No 46134 *The Cheshire Regiment* blows off as it approaches Carlisle past Upperby Yard at the head of the Birmingham New Street–Glasgow Central, which was normally a Pacific working. The date is 9 August 1960, at which time the locomotive was allocated to Crewe North. Rebuilt in December 1953, it would last only nine years as a rebuild, being withdrawn in December 1962 from Carlisle Upperby, having covered only around 470,000 miles in rebuilt form. *Gavin Morrison*

Right: No 46160 *Queen Victoria's Rifleman* alongside Carlisle Kingmoor shed, ready to leave on a special on 28 November 1964. *Gavin Morrison*

Above: No 46107 *Argyll and Sutherland Highlander* was one of five rebuilt 'Royal Scots' to spend all its rebuilt days allocated to Polmadie shed at Glasgow. (The others were Nos 46102/4/5/21.) It is shown here, two months after its last general overhaul, awaiting its next duty at Carlisle Kingmoor shed. Rebuilt in February 1950, it would be withdrawn, along with all the other Scottish-allocated members of the class, in December 1962. As with other Scottish-allocated 'Royal Scots', its mileage in service was much lower than that of its English-based sisters. *Gavin Morrison*

Right: After 11 years in rebuilt form working from Leeds Holbeck shed on the Scottish expresses over the Settle & Carlisle line, No 46133 *The Green Howards* was transferred south to Kentish Town to work on the southern section of the Midland main line. In dirty condition but with a clean 'Palatine' headboard, it is seen approaching Hendon on 20 July 1959. Rebuilt in July 1944, it would end its days at Newton Heath, in February 1963.
K. L. Cook / Rail Archive Stephenson

No 46106 *Gordon Highlander* is shown at the unusual location (for a rebuilt 'Royal Scot') of Wellingborough shed on 20 August 1961, when it was allocated to Derby. It had received its last overhaul — a heavy intermediate — in May, and was looking in reasonable condition. *K. Fairey*

In very dirty condition, No 46148 *The Manchester Regiment* leaves
Kettering with an express for St Pancras during the summer of
1961. Whilst working the Midland main line it was allocated to
Sheffield Millhouses (41C). *G. D. King*

Above: In fine external condition No 46143 *The South Staffordshire Regiment* passes the disused ticket platform north of Knighton Tunnel, Leicester, with a Friday-afternoon relief Manchester–St Pancras express in July 1961. This was one of approximately 25 rebuilt 'Patriots' and 'Royal Scots' allocated to sheds that worked expresses on the Midland main line south of Leeds at the beginning of the 1960s. Rebuilt in June 1949, it would end its days at Annesley (on the Great Central), in December 1963. *G. D. King*

Right: No 46133 *The Green Howards* climbs out of Sheffield up the 1-in-100 bank to Broadway Tunnel past Millhouses and Eccleshall in 1959, when the locomotive was allocated to Kentish Town shed (14B). *D. Penney*

Left: A fine action shot of No 46140 *The King's Royal Rifle Corps* climbing the 5½ miles of 1 in 100 from Sheffield to Dore, passing Millhouses, with an up express on 5 March 1960, when it was allocated to Kentish Town. The smokebox has received some attention, but the rest of the locomotive is in terrible external condition. It visited Crewe Works in April 1960 for a heavy intermediate repair and would end its working days at Longsight in October 1965, before being scrapped by J. McWilliam at Shettleston in March 1966. *D. Marriott*

Below: Another view of No 46140 *The King's Royal Rifle Corps* at the top of the 1-in-100 climb out of Sheffield at Dore & Totley as it heads for Broadway Tunnel on 3 October 1959. *D. Marriott*

Left: No 46164 *The Artists' Rifleman* seen in terrible external condition just south of Healey station, on the 5.30pm express from Sheffield to Manchester on 9 August 1961, whilst allocated to Millhouses. It would be withdrawn in December 1962 and scrapped at Crewe Works in March 1963. *D. Marriott*

Below: No 46157 *The Royal Artilleryman* heads the 3.30pm Newcastle–Birmingham just south of Healey on the climb out of Sheffield to Dore. The date was 4 July 1961, and the locomotive was looking in fine external condition following repaint during its general repair in May 1961. It was allocated to Saltley at the time, but in June 1962 it moved to Carlisle Upperby and then Kingmoor before being withdrawn in January 1964 and scrapped at Crewe Works in February 1964. *D. Marriott*

Left: Another very fine picture taken on the climb out of Sheffield on the 1-in-100 gradient to Broadway Tunnel shows No 46132 *The King's Regiment, Liverpool* at the head of a Leeds City–St Pancras express in the late 1950s, when the locomotive was allocated to Kentish Town. Rebuilt in November 1943, it would be withdrawn in February 1964 from Carlisle Kingmoor shed. *D. Penney*

Above: No 46106 *Gordon Highlander* hurries through Bromsgrove at the bottom of the 1-in-37 Lickey Incline with an express for the South. By 1962, when the picture was taken, the locomotive was allocated to Derby. *J. Edgington*

Left: In the early 1960s, after Saltley shed received a few rebuilt 'Scots' on its allocation, they were occasionally seen at Bath Green Park shed. No 46160 *Queen Victoria's Rifleman*, showing a 21A (Saltley) shedplate, awaits its return working north at Bath shed on 1 July 1961. Inside the shed is Great Western pannier tank No 3742. Rebuilt in February 1945, the 'Scot' would be one of the last to be withdrawn, in May 1965 from Carlisle Kingmoor shed. *R. C. Riley*

Above: On 23 March 1961 the down 'Waverley' (St Pancras-Edinburgh) passes through the southern suburbs of Leeds at Stourton, headed by Nottingham-allocated No 46118 *Royal Welch Fusilier*. Rebuilt in December 1946, this locomotive would be withdrawn from Carlisle Upperby shed in June 1964 having covered 2,092,730 miles in service, including around 894,000 in rebuilt form by 31 December 1963. *Gavin Morrison*

On Sundays the 12.45pm from Leeds to Liverpool was usually single-headed, and on 28 February 1960 No 46124 *London Scottish* of Edge Hill was in charge, being shown ready to leave Leeds City. Following rebuilding in December 1943 it was allocated to Edge Hill all the time except for its final two months and was a frequent performer on trans-Pennine expresses. *Gavin Morrison*

No 46108 *Seaforth Highlander* was the third member of the class to be rebuilt, in August 1943, and was then allocated to Leeds Holbeck for working the Scottish expresses over the Settle & Carlisle. Here it is shown climbing out of Leeds, on the now abandoned section of the LNWR route to Farnley, heading a summer relief (12.35 Leeds City–Manchester) on 10 August 1961. This locomotive would be the first of Holbeck's original rebuilds to be transferred away, in December 1962, and would be withdrawn from Carlisle Upperby in January 1963. *Gavin Morrison*

Above: On Sunday 24 May 1959 the morning Newcastle–Liverpool trans-Pennine express heads away from Huddersfield behind No 46155 *The Lancer*. It is passing Gledholt Junction, where trains could be crossed over between the fast and slow lines. (The fast lines were taken out of use about 20 years ago.) No 46155 would be the last rebuilt 'Scot' allocated to Crewe North shed, before being transferred away to Holyhead on 24 August 1963. *Gavin Morrison*

Right: Whilst the rebuilt 'Scots' were a daily sight on the trans-Pennine line via Huddersfield, they were rarely seen on the Calder

Valley route even when a few were allocated to Low Moor prior to withdrawal. The famous Heaton–Red Bank empty newspaper train provided a wide variety of motive power combinations and on 18 July 1961 produced Holbeck's No 46117 *Welsh Guardsman* piloting Stanier Class 5 No 45494. The lengthy train, usually consisting of around 22 vans, is shown passing through Sowerby Bridge, heading for Manchester. After rebuilding in December 1943, No 46117 spent all its time at Holbeck, apart from a few months at the end of its career at Mirfield, where it did little work. Withdrawal came in November 1962. *Gavin Morrison*

Left: Leeds Holbeck was the first shed to receive rebuilt 'Scots', and they will always be remembered for their work on the Scottish expresses over the Settle & Carlisle. No 46117 *Welsh Guardsman* was the fourth member of the class to arrive at Holbeck in March 1944 and remained allocated to Holbeck almost until its withdrawal in November 1962. It is shown at its home shed awaiting its next duty on 4 October 1962, just before it was transferred to Mirfield for a month. Earlier in its career, on 18 April 1952, this locomotive was involved in a serious accident whilst working the up 'Thames–Clyde Express' at Blea Moor: whilst being piloted by Midland Compound No 41040, which was the cause of the accident, it was derailed at about 50mph and landed on its side. It duly received a heavy general repair and was back in traffic by 10 June 1952. *Gavin Morrison*

Right: A rebuilt 'Scot' at the head of the 'Thames–Clyde Express', a train with which the class will always be associated. No 46145 *The Duke of Wellington's Regt (West Riding)* prepares to leave Leeds City on its journey north to Glasgow St Enoch on 28 February 1960. *Gavin Morrison*

Left: After 32 years allocated to sheds on the West Coast main line, No 46100 *Royal Scot* was transferred to Nottingham shed (16A) on 7 November 1959, along with two other rebuilt 'Scots' and a rebuilt 'Patriot'. On 23 October 1961 it was a rare performer on the 3.14pm Leeds–Morecambe slow train, and is shown passing Wortley Junction, about one mile from Leeds City station. The now demolished bridge carrying the Great Northern main line into Leeds Central can just be seen in the background. *Royal Scot* had been rebuilt in June 1950 and would become one of the first of the class to be withdrawn, in October 1962, having received its last general repair in December 1957. *Gavin Morrison*

Below: No 46109 *Royal Engineer* was the second of the class to be rebuilt, in July 1943; it was then sent to Leeds Holbeck to work the Scottish expresses over the Settle & Carlisle and would remain there for over 19 years until withdrawn in December 1962. It is shown heading the down 'Waverley' round the sharp curve at Shipley on 20 April 1961, not long before the BR/Sulzer Type 4 'Peaks' took over these duties. Platforms have now been installed on both lines at the side of the Shipley triangle. *Gavin Morrison*

Below: A view of the southbound 'Waverley' express negotiating the sharp curve at Shipley Bingley Junction on 10 May 1961, headed by Holbeck's longtime-allocated No 46117 *Welsh Guardsman*. The lines on the extreme left, to Bradford Forster Square, have now been singled. *Gavin Morrison*

Right: No 46113 *Cameronian* was allocated to Leeds Holbeck for 10 years between May 1951 and October 1961, when it was transferred away to Low Moor and Mirfield for its last year of service.

It had obviously been borrowed by Leeds Holbeck on 10 May 1962 to work the evening Leeds–Morecambe residential and made a fine sight heading north between Bingley and Crossflats. The former Holbeck 'Scots' transferred to Low Moor and Mirfield did very little work, and it is possible that this was *Cameronian*'s last main-line express working. Rebuilt in December 1950, it received its last general repair in April 1957 and would be withdrawn in December 1962. Note Mirfield's 56D shedplate and the fact that the tender still had the old lion-and-wheel emblem. *Gavin Morrison*

Left: Saturday 13 February 1965 was the day chosen by the Lancashire & North West branch of the Railway Correspondence & Travel Society to run the 'Rebuilt Scot' commemorative railtour, which left Crewe at 9.15am for Carlisle via the Settle & Carlisle. When the booked locomotive, No 46160 *Queen Victoria's Rifleman*, failed, No 46115 *Scots Guardsman* was substituted at the last minute, and credit must be given to Crewe North shed for its fine external appearance and wooden nameplate. A stop for water was made at Hellifield, where this picture was taken, but surprisingly another stop for the same reason had to be made at Settle. As well as being the first of the class to be fitted with smoke-deflectors by the LMS, in 1947, following rebuild in August of that year, this locomotive would be the last to be withdrawn, in January 1966, finishing up at the Keighley & Worth Valley Railway at the start of its career in preservation. *Gavin Morrison*

Above: In the last years of steam the 3.40pm Bradford Forster Square–Carlisle stopping train was a particular favourite with enthusiasts, as it often produced a rebuilt 'Scot', 'Patriot' or 'Britannia'. On 3 April 1965 No 46152 *The King's Dragoon Guardsman* climbs past Stainforth towards Blea Moor. *P. J. Fitton*

Left: A fine picture of Holbeck's No 46113 *Cameronian* as it pulls away from Dumfries for Glasgow St Enoch on what would be the 10.35am departure from Leeds City on 13 June 1959. In the background, in the bay platforms, can be seen a railtour headed by ex-Great North of Scotland 4-4-0 *Gordon Highlander* (not to be confused with rebuilt 'Scot' No 46106). Also visible, on the right of the picture, is one of the local '2P' 4-4-0s. *D. Penney*

Above: With the help of a Fairburn 2-6-4T at the rear, Polmadie-allocated No 46102 *Black Watch* makes excellent progress up Beattock Bank past Greskine on 4 June 1960. Allocated to Polmadie for its entire career in rebuilt form (from October 1949), it would be withdrawn in December 1962, along with the other Scottish Region members of the class. It covered only around 425,000 miles in rebuilt form up to the end of 1957. *Gavin Morrison*

Above: With the old A74 main road in the foreground, No 46105 *Cameron Highlander* catches the late-evening light as it starts to descend Beattock Bank at the head of the 4pm Glasgow Central–Manchester Victoria express on 20 May 1961 — three months after the locomotive received its last general overhaul at Crewe. Transferred to Polmadie in February 1943, five years before rebuilding, it would remain allocated there until withdrawal in December 1962, prior to scrapping by J. McWilliam at Shettleston in May 1964. *Gavin Morrison*

Right: Pictured at the head of an up working from Glasgow to Manchester on 14 October 1961, No 46142 *The York & Lancaster Regiment* heads southbound at Lamington on the ascent towards Beattock Summit on the ex-Caledonian Railway main line. At this date the locomotive was allocated, appropriately, to Newton Heath in Manchester, being transferred to Longsight on 22 June 1963, from where it would be withdrawn in January 1964. *Derek Cross*

Above: No 46132 *The King's Regiment, Liverpool* appears to have paid a recent visit to works as it heads south near Crawford on a seven-coach train on 14 July 1962. The bridge in the background carries the old A74 main road to Glasgow, since upgraded to become the M74. *Gavin Morrison*

Right: Once its days of working the West Coast main line were over, No 46164 *The Artists' Rifleman* was transferred to Millhouses shed at Sheffield c1960 and ultimately to Annesley for Great Central duties; it is seen at Belgrave & Birstall with an afternoon Nottingham Victoria–Marylebone semi-fast on 27 July 1963. Rebuilt in June 1951, it would be withdrawn with 23 other members of the class in December 1962. *G. D. King*

Above: On 23 September 1963 there was a special working from Farnley Junction (55C) shed, Leeds, to Crewe Works, when the last of the original Holbeck-allocated rebuilt 'Scots' departed. These were Nos 46109/30/45, all of which had been withdrawn in December 1962, but No 46145 was steamed for the occasion, and hauled the other two over the Pennines to Crewe. In dismal conditions the trio prepare to leave Farnley Junction shed. *Gavin Morrison*

Right: After No 46100 *Royal Scot* was withdrawn in October 1962, it was purchased by Billy Butlin and taken to his holiday camp at Skegness, where it was exhibited on a plinth. It remained at Skegness for many years, before being sold again and moving to Bressingham Steam Museum in Norfolk, where it remains to this day. It has not left Bressingham since its arrival and is painted in LMS red livery, which it never carried in rebuilt form. These pictures show the nameplate and the locomotive on its plinth at Skegness in August 1963. *Both G. Rixon*

ROYAL SCOT

PRIOR TO CONVERSION
THIS LOCOMOTIVE WITH THE ROYAL SCOT TRAIN WAS EXHIBITED AT THE CENTURY OF PROGRESS
EXPOSITION, CHICAGO, 1933, AND MADE A TOUR OF THE DOMINION OF CANADA AND THE UNITED
STATES OF AMERICA. THE ENGINE AND TRAIN COVERED 11,194 MILES OVER THE RAILROADS
OF THE NORTH AMERICAN CONTINENT AND WAS INSPECTED BY 3,021,601 PEOPLE.
W. GILBERTSON — DRIVER.   T. BLACKETT — FIREMAN.
J. JACKSON — FIREMAN.   W. C. WOODS — FITTER.

Above: After withdrawal in January 1966, No 46115 *Scots Guardsman* passed into preservation and was taken to the Keighley & Worth Valley Railway. Eventually it moved to the Dinting Preservation Centre, and after several years of effort was restored to working order, it is seen on 26 June 1976, prior to the fitting of smoke-deflectors. *Gavin Morrison*

Right: No 46115 *Scots Guardsman* enjoying its first main-line outing on 21 September 1978. This was followed by another on 11 November 1978, which turned out to be its last working to date. It is currently at The Railway Age, Crewe, and the hope remains that it will return to main-line duties. It is seen climbing the bank near Chinley *en route* from Guide Bridge to York on 11 November 1978, painted in LMS post-1946 lined black; as such it is the only member of the class to have carried this livery when fitted with smoke-deflectors. *Gavin Morrison*

A fascinating picture showing part of the display of nameplates organised by Ian Wright of Sheffield at a private museum at Fawley on 27 July 1997. There are 19 rebuilt 'Scot' nameplates in the picture. The current value of the plates probably exceeds the cost of the locomotives when originally built. *H. Ballantyne*

Summary of Rebuilt 'Royal Scots'

LMS No	BR No	Name	Built	Rebuilt	Withdrawn	Disposal	Scrapped
(6100)	46100	Royal Scot	7/27	6/50	10/62	Preservation	-
6101	46101	Royal Scots Grey	8/27	11/45	8/63	Slag Reduction, Rotherham	4/64
(6102)	46102	Black Watch	8/27	10/49-	12/62	J. McWilliam, Shettleston	5/64
6103	46103	Royal Scots Fusilier	8/27	6/43	12/62	Crewe Works	9/63
6104	46104	Scottish Borderer	8/27	3/46	12/62	J. McWilliam, Shettleston	5/64
(6105)	46105	Cameron Highlander	8/27	5/48	12/62	J. McWilliam, Shettleston	5/64
(6106)	46106	Gordon Highlander	8/27	9/49	12/62	Crewe Works	4/63
(6107)	46107	Argyll and Sutherland Highlander	8/27	2/50	12/62	J. McWilliam, Shettleston	5/64
6108	46108	Seaforth Highlander	8/27	8/43	1/63	Crewe Works	5/63
6109	46109	Royal Engineer	9/27	7/43	12/62	Crewe Works	12/63
(6110)	46110	Grenadier Guardsman	9/27	1/53	2/64	J. McWilliam, Shettleston	12/64
6111	46111	Royal Fusilier	9/27	10/47	9/63	Crewe Works	11/63
6112	46112	Sherwood Forester	9/27	9/43	5/64	J. Cashmore Ltd, Great Bridge	9/64
(6113)	46113	Cameronian	9/27	12/50	12/62	Crewe Works	6/63
6114	46114	Coldstream Guardsman	9/27	6/46	9/63	Slag Reduction, Rotherham	4/64
6115	46115	Scots Guardsman	9/27	8/47	1/66	Preservation	-
6116	46116	Irish Guardsman	9/27	5/44	8/63	Crewe Works	9/63
6117	46117	Welsh Guardsman	10/27	12/43	11/62	Crewe Works	12/63
6118	46118	Royal Welch Fusilier	10/27	12/46	6/64	J. N. Connell, Coatbridge	11/64
6119	46119	Lancashire Fusilier	10/27	9/44	11/63	Crewe Works	11/63
6120	46120	Royal Inniskilling Fusilier	10/27	11/44	7/63	Crewe Works	10/63
6121	46121	Highland Light Infantry, City of Glasgow Regiment	10/27	8/46	12/62	J. McWilliam, Shettleston	5/64
6122	46122	Royal Ulster Rifleman	10/27	9/45	10/64	A. Draper, Hull	2/65
(6123)	46123	Royal Irish Fusilier	10/27	5/49	11/62	Crewe Works	4/63
6124	46124	London Scottish	11/27	12/43	12/62	Crewe Works	4/63
6125	46125	3rd Carabinier	8/27	8/43	10/64	J. Cashmore Ltd, Great Bridge	1/65
6126	46126	Royal Army Service Corps	8/27	6/45	10/63	Crewe Works	11/63
6127	46127	Old Contemptibles	8/27	8/44	12/62	Crewe Works	5/63
6128	46128	The Lovat Scouts	8/27	6/46	5/65	Motherwell Machinery & Scrap Co	7/65
6129	46129	The Scottish Horse	8/27	12/44	6/64	Central Wagon Co, Ince, Wigan	11/64
(6130)	46130	The West Yorkshire Regiment	8/27	12/49	12/62	Crewe Works	10/63
6131	46131	The Royal Warwickshire Regiment	9/27	10/44	11/62	Crewe Works	11/62
6132	46132	The King's Regiment, Liverpool	9/27	11/43	2/64	West of Scotland Shipbreaking Co, Troon	4/65
6133	46133	The Green Howards	9/27	7/44	2/63	Crewe Works	5/63
(6134)	46134	The Cheshire Regiment	9/27	12/53	12/62	Crewe Works	4/63
6135	46135	The East Lancashire Regiment	9/27	1/47	12/62	Crewe Works	4/63
(6136)	46136	The Border Regiment	9/27	3/50	3/64	Crewe Works	4/64
(6137)	46137	The Prince of Wales' Volunteers (South Lancashire)	9/27	3/55	11/62	Crewe Works	5/63
6138	46138	The London Irish Rifleman	9/27	6/44	2/63	Crewe Works	5/63
6139	46139	The Welch Regiment	10/27	11/46	10/62	Crewe Works	5/63
(6140)	46140	The King's Royal Rifle Corps	10/27	5/52	10/65	J. McWilliam, Shettleston	3/66
6141	46141	The North Staffordshire Regiment	10/27	10/50	4/64	Crewe Works	7/64
(6142)	46142	The York & Lancaster Regiment	10/27	2/51	1/64	Crewe Works	1/64
(6143)	46143	The South Staffordshire Regiment	10/27	6/49	12/63	Crewe Works	1/64
6144	46144	Honourable Artillery Company	10/27	6/45	1/64	Crewe Works	1/64
6145	46145	The Duke of Wellington's Regt. (West Riding)	10/27	1/44	12/62	Crewe Works	10/63
6146	46146	The Rifle Brigade	10/27	10/43	12/62	Crewe Works	3/63
6147	46147	The Northamptonshire Regiment	10/27	9/46	12/62	Crewe Works	3/63
(6148)	46148	The Manchester Regiment	11/27	7/54	11/64	Bird Group, Morriston	1/65
6149	46149	The Middlesex Regiment	11/27	4/45	8/63	Crewe Works	11/63
6150	46150	The Life Guardsman	5/30	12/45	12/62	Crewe Works	12/63
(6151)	46151	The Royal Horse Guardsman	6/30	4/53	12/62	Crewe Works	8/63
6152	46152	The King's Dragoon Guardsman	7/30	8/45	4/65	Motherwell Machinery & Scrap Co	7/65
(6153)	46153	The Royal Dragoon	7/30	8/49	12/62	Crewe Works	5/63
6154	46154	The Hussar	7/30	3/48	3/63	Crewe Works	3/63
6155	46155	The Lancer	7/30	8/50	12/64	West of Scotland Shipbreaking Co, Troon	2/65
(6156)	46156	The South Wales Borderer	7/30	5/54	10/64	A. Draper, Hull	2/65
6157	46157	The Royal Artilleryman	8/30	1/46	1/64	Bird Group, Risca	2/64
6158	46158	The Loyal Regiment	8/30	9/52	10/63	Crewe Works	11/63
6159	46159	The Royal Air Force	8/30	10/45	12/62	T. W. Ward Ltd, Beighton	3/65
6160	46160	Queen Victoria's Rifleman	9/30	2/45	5/65	West of Scotland Shipbreaking Co, Troon	12/64
6161	46161	King's Own	9/30	10/46	11/62	Crewe Works	5/64
(6162)	46162	Queen's Westminster Rifleman	9/30	1/48	5/64	J. N. Connell, Coatbridge	9/64
(6163)	46163	Civil Service Rifleman	9/30	10/53	8/64	Bird Group, Risca	2/65
6164	46164	The Artists Rifleman	9/30	6/51	12/62	Crewe Works	3/63
6165	46165	The Ranger (12th London Regt.)	10/30	6/52	11/64	T. W. Ward Ltd, Beighton	3/65
6166	46166	London Rifle Brigade	10/30	1/45	9/64	West of Scotland Shipbreaking Co, Troon	12/64
(6167)	46167	The Hertfordshire Regiment	10/30	12/48	4/64	Motherwell Machinery & Scrap Co	5/64
6168	46168	The Girl Guide	10/30	4/46	5/64	Crewe Works	8/64
6169	46169	The Boy Scout	11/30	5/45	5/63	Crewe Works	8/63
6170	46170	British Legion	12/29	11/35	12/62	Crewe Works	1/63

Front cover: A superb picture of No 46108 *Seaforth Highlander* heading north in fine style at Morecambe South Junction, just north of Lancaster. This locomotive was the third member of the class to be rebuilt, in August 1943, and was allocated to Leeds Holbeck, for working over the Settle & Carlisle. It was reallocated away from Holbeck in December 1952 and thereafter spent the rest of its days on the West Coast main line, being finally withdrawn in January 1963 from Carlisle Upperby shed. *D. Penney*

Back cover: A Warwickshire Railway Society special alongside Carlisle Kingmoor shed on 28 November 1964, with a very well-cleaned No 46160 *Queen Victoria's Rifleman* ready to head south. The locomotive is believed to have been fitted with replica wooden nameplates specially for the occasion; note also the yellow line on the cabside, indicating that the locomotive was banned from working under the electric wires south of Crewe. Rebuilt in February 1945, it was one of the last to be withdrawn, in May 1965 from Carlisle Kingmoor shed, having received its last general repair as late as October 1961. *Gavin Morrison*

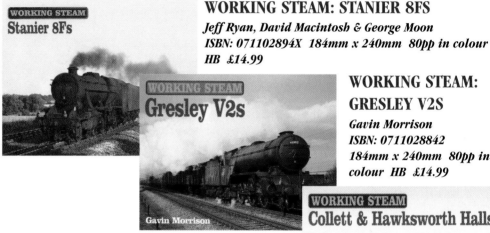